Praise for
Growing Figs in Cold Clima

Growing Figs in Cold Climates is a welcome addition to our library
from Lee Reich, our fruit guru. We have grown this delicious fruit
on Maine's chilly coast, but Lee shows us how to do it even better.

—Barbara Damrosch and Eliot Coleman, farmers,
Four Season Farm, authors

How far insightful horticultural knowledge can take us! Lee Reich
has just talked me into trying to grow figs. Plant wisdom thrives
in *Growing Figs in Cold Climates*. Clear instruction, backed with
appropriate choice of methods for one's location, opens the doors
on fig potential. Truly, to eat a fresh fig is to dine with the gods.

—Michael Phillips, Holistic Orchard Network, author,
The Apple Grower and *The Holistic Orchard*

All gardeners need to take a look at *Growing Figs in Cold Climates*
by Lee Reich. There is so much information applicable to growing any fruit that even if you don't want to grow figs, you won't
regret the read. Here is an example of the perfect "how-to" gardening book. It is clearly written, with so many beautiful photos
and expertly drawn illustrations, it could be a coffee table book
and not just the next have-to-have gardening book. By all means,
add *Growing Figs in Cold Climates* to the Lee Reich shelf in your
bookcase. If you don't have such a collection get on it, ASAP!

—Jeff Lowenfels, Lord of the Roots, author,
DIY Autoflowering Cannabis

For those who like to push the standard boundaries of suggested growing zones, Lee Reich's tribute to the mighty fig is a monumental and easily digestible resource. From pruning to pests to pairings, Reich's open love letter to the fig is full of insider tips on how to bring the familiar taste of the Mediterranean closer to home. Warning: There may be a Brown Turkey or Italian Honey in your hoop house future!

—Jules Torti, editor-in-chief, *Harrowsmith* magazine, author,
Trail Mix: 920km on the Camino de Santiago

Happily for fruit lovers, expert grower Lee Reich has turned his attention to figs. This latest volume offers multiple methods for producing a bountiful fig harvest in frigid climes, even without a greenhouse. You'll learn how to grow the luscious fruit in containers or in the ground, how to prune judiciously, choose the right cultivar, and much more. This detailed guide is yet another of Reich's indispensable additions to the gardener's bookshelf. Be sure to add it to your own library.

—Rebecca Martin, *Mother Earth News* magazine

Finally, a complete book about *Growing Figs in Cold Climates*. Lee Reich is a master at growing food, especially fruits, and his extensive personal knowledge about figs comes through clearly in his writings. This book covers every aspect and even shows you how to grow figs in five different ways to meet every gardener's needs. I've been following Lee's work for some time and trust what he says. He has a rare knack for combining science and practicality to come up with a simple way to garden. Follow his advice for growing figs and you are guaranteed success.

—Robert Pavlis, author, *Garden Myths, Building Natural Ponds,* and
Soil Science for Gardeners, owner, Aspen Grove Gardens

For a cold climate grower like me who does not yet grow figs. Lee Reich has made it seem easy and given me a fig growing goal. Some of his five techniques to grow figs way outside their usual growing areas would apply to other fruit as well, expanding the list of fruit to grow in your backyard or homestead. Plus the techniques open up vast areas of the planet to growing fresh figs. Finally Lee's FIGurative puns put a jovial touch to the text.

—Stefan Sobkowiak, The Permaculture Orchard YouTube Channel

Lee Reich has written *the* definitive fig book! If you want to experience the bliss of eating a perfectly ripe fig fresh from your own tree—a delight that has to be experienced to be believed— this book will show you how. If you thought your climate was too cold for figs, his clear and well-illustrated instructions on different methods for overwintering fig trees will change your mind. With detailed information on the biology of these unique trees and on the types of figs, along with clear instructions on how to prune them, there is plenty here for novice and experienced fig growers alike.

—Linda Gilkeson, author, *Backyard Bounty*

Growing Figs
in Cold Climates

A COMPLETE GUIDE

LEE REICH

Lee Reich

new society
PUBLISHERS

Cover design by Diane McIntosh.
All photos taken by author unless otherwise noted.

Printed in Canada. First printing September, 2021.

Inquiries regarding requests to reprint all or part of *Growing Figs in Cold Climates* should be addressed to New Society Publishers at the address below. To order directly from the publishers, please call toll-free (North America) 1-800-567-6772, or order online at www.new society.com

Any other inquiries can be directed by mail to:
New Society Publishers
P.O. Box 189, Gabriola Island, BC
V0R 1X0, Canada
(250) 247-9737

LIBRARY AND ARCHIVES CANADA CATALOGUING IN PUBLICATION
Title: Growing figs in cold climates : a complete guide / Lee Reich.
Names: Reich, Lee, author.
Description: Includes index.
Identifiers: Canadiana (print) 20210264950 | Canadiana (ebook) 20210266686 | ISBN 9780865719576
   (softcover) | ISBN 9781550927504 (PDF) | ISBN 9781771423465 (EPUB)
Subjects: LCSH: Fig. | LCSH: Fig—Effect of cold on.
Classification: LCC SB365 .R45 2021 | DDC 634/.37—dc23

Funded by the Government of Canada | Financé par le gouvernement du Canada

New Society Publishers' mission is to publish books that contribute in fundamental ways to building an ecologically sustainable and just society, and to do so with the least possible impact on the environment, in a manner that models this vision.

FSC MIX Paper from responsible sources FSC® C016245

Certified B Corporation

new society PUBLISHERS

Mmmmmmm

TABLE OF CONTENTS

San Piero fig, breba crop

INTRODUCTION

*W*HAT IS IT ABOUT FIG TREES that makes so many people want to grow them? And that includes many people who you'd imagine wouldn't think of growing figs because they garden where winters seem to be too cold and summers seem *not* hot enough for this exotic fruit. I happen to be one of those people. Fig was the first fruit I planted many years ago when I began gardening. I was living in Madison, Wisconsin, where winter temperatures regularly plummeted to minus 25 degrees Fahrenheit! (-32°C!)

Perhaps the widespread appeal of figs speaks to our geographic and cultural roots. The plant originated in the searing heat and arid climate of the Middle East, one of the cradles of civilization. It was first cultivated in southern Arabia, possibly in Neolithic times. King Urukagina of Mesopotamia was a fan.

The Bible offers further "evidence" of fig's widespread appeal. Fig has often been used to portray the Tree of Knowledge. It was the first clothing for Adam and Eve: "And the eyes of them both were opened, and they knew that they were naked; and they sewed fig leaves together, and made themselves aprons."

Fig is the most mentioned fruit in the Bible. It's also one of the two sacred fruits of Islam and figures prominently, as well, in Greek mythology.

This fruit's appeal also speaks to our more recent roots. Throughout the world, fig trees grace the yards of first, second, even third generation Italians, Greeks, Lebanese, and others of Mediterranean descent.

Primitive and ethnic roots aside, eyes light up pretty much everywhere when the prospect of being able to grow and harvest fresh figs is presented. It's the flavor! And the texture! (Or as food scientists like to say, its "organoleptic" quality, a 50-cent word melding together a food's flavor, texture, and anything else that contributes to its enjoyment.) A fresh fig is a totally different gustatory experience from a dried fig. Fresh, the fruit is soft and juicy, with a honey sweet, rich flavor. Each variety, of which there are many, differs slightly in their organoleptic profile.

If you already grow figs, this book will help you grow better or more figs, or be able to manage them more easily. If you haven't yet experienced the rewards of growing figs, you have a treat in store for you. Read on, and learn how to grow figs in cold climates.

Opposite: Adam and Eve, Titian (ca. 1550)

1

WHY YOU CAN GROW FIGS
IN COLD CLIMATES

To IMAGINE THE CONDITIONS under which a fig tree really thrives, picture an Arabian courtyard *in summer*. There stands a fig tree, basking in abundant, hot sunshine. Hmm... I wrote, above, that figs can be grown in cold climates. What's up?

Heat and sun are what a fig thrives on in summer. Winter is another story. Many cold areas of the world—interior North America and eastern Europe, for example—host a continental climate, cold in winter but usually hot and sunny in summer. The hottest and most humid weather I ever experienced was in Wisconsin, even though that extreme lasted only a few weeks.

The Wisconsin climate is just one kind of cold climate. There are others, which I'll get to later on, at least in so far as those climates relate to growing figs.

Here's a summary of the reasons you can grow figs in your cold climate:

- Fig is a subtropical plant that tolerates temperatures well below freezing.
- The plant enjoys a winter rest.

- The plant is leafless during that winter rest.
- Pollination is unnecessary.
- Fig has a unique fruit-bearing habit.
- And, fig plants tolerate abuse.

Let me elaborate.

Fig is a very adaptable plant, and can be grown well beyond its original home for a number of reasons. For starters, it's not a tropical plant. It's *a subtropical plant, tolerating subfreezing temperatures*—typically down into the low 'teens (about -10°C, USDA Cold Hardiness Zone 8), more or less depending on the particular variety. A fig tree actually *enjoys a winter rest at cold temperatures*. And it does so in the nude, *leafless in winter*, so light is unnecessary during that period. As such, it can be buried or packed away in dark storage for winter, another trait that makes it easier for us cold climate growers to grow figs. No need for a warm greenhouse. Or any greenhouse.

Most fruit plants need pollination to set fruit. In some cases, self-pollination suffices; in others cross-pollination is necessary, with pollen supplied by a different clone or variety of the same kind of fruit. Not to worry when growing figs; most varieties of this ever-adaptable plant don't need any pollination (neither self- nor cross-pollination) at all to bear fruit!

Botanically, a "fig fruit" is a synconium, which is essentially inside-out stem tissue with flowers lining its insides. (Botanically, the actual fig fruits are all the little, round drupelets on the inside of what we usually call the "fig fruit.")

Far from the shores of the Middle East, what we usually grow are varieties of "Common" type figs. Common type fig varieties, true to their name, are the category to which most fig varieties belong, and they bear fruits without pollination.

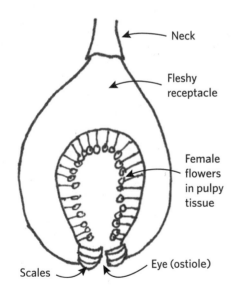

Neck

Fleshy receptacle

Female flowers in pulpy tissue

Scales

Eye (ostiole)

Diagram of fig "fruit"

Beyond the fig's natural habitat we might also grow one of the relatively few "San Pedro" type fig varieties, which bear a breba, or early, crop without pollination, but usually need pollination for the later, main crop. (These two crops will be explained shortly.) The important point for us cold-climate fig growers, is that *pollination is unnecessary*.

For completeness, allow me to mention a third type of fig, "Smyrna" type, which will not bear any fruit without pollination.

Let me digress

For figs that need cross-pollination, the sexual act is interesting but not so simple. A special wasp, known as *Blastophaga psenes,* must get in on the act to effect the transfer of pollen. Female *B. psenes* wasps spend much of their life inside a caprifig, emerging only when she's ready to go out in the world to find a new caprifig in which to lay her eggs. As *Ms. B. psenes* makes her exit, she inadvertently rubs against and picks up pollen from the male flowers.

In commercial settings, caprifig fruits are harvested and hung among branches of trees in Smyrna type fig orchards. There, emerging wasps seek out and enter what's available, Smyrna type figs, in which to lay their eggs.

Unfortunately for the tiny wasp, the structure of the Smyrna type fig flower is such that she cannot lay her eggs. As she scurries around inside the fruit, frustrated in her attempt to lay eggs, she unknowingly transfers the pollen from the caprifig to

Blastophagus psenes, female

the female flower of the Smyrna type fig. And fruits develop.

All very interesting and sad (for the *B. psenes* wasps) but of no practical use to us cold climate fig growers. Which is fortunate because this is another feature that eases fig growing in cold climates. No need to raise caprifigs just for their pollen or maintain a herd of *B. psenes* wasps.

In the case of Smyrna type figs and the main crop of San Pedro figs, cross-pollination is needed, and the pollen for that sexual exchange must come from a special type of fig known as a caprifig. Caprifigs are inedible but do have male flowers.

FRUIT BEARING HABIT

A peach tree bears fruits on one-year-old stems, that is, stems that grew the previous season. An apple tree usually bears fruit on stems two, three, or more years old. Most fruits that grow in cold or even frigid climates are borne on stems that grew one or more years' previously.

Figs are rather *unique among fruit plants in their bearing habit*. A fig tree might bear fruit on new, growing shoots; on one-year-old stems; or on both new, growing shoots and on one-year-old stems. This is yet another reason that figs are adaptable to cold climate growing—there's not necessarily a need to have stems survive winter in order to get a crop the following season. You can cut back stems in order to more easily protect them from cold or to make it easier to move the whole plant to a protected winter home. How your plant bears fruit depends on both the variety and how you prune it.

A nice offshoot (sic) of this bearing habit, for fig lovers/growers everywhere, is that fig plants are very quick to come into bearing. I've had plants bear the season after I rooted them from cuttings!

Many fig varieties potentially bear two crops each year. First to ripen is the breba crop, borne on one-year-old stems. The so-called main crop ripens later, developing in leaf axils of new, growing shoots. The fruit of the breba crop and the main crop might differ in appearance, size, and flavor.

The whole breba crop ripens more or less contemporaneously. In contrast to the breba crop and to most tree fruits, a fig's main crop ripens over a long period. New fruits keep forming at the

First year plant; figs bear quickly!

This season's breba crop
beginning to form on last
season's wood

ends of growing stems as older fruits, lower down along the stem, are ripening—until growth is slowed or arrested by insufficient light, warmth, water, or fertility. Fruit buds that do not yield main crop figs one season can give rise to the following season's breba crop, if that variety is one that bears a breba crop.

"Main" crop forming on new shoot

THE FIG TREE

Let's not become so focused on the delectable fruit that we ignore the tree itself. After all, a trunk (or trunks) and leafy stems are needed for places on which to hang fruit as well as for shuttling nutrients around and harnessing sunlight for growth and good tasting fruit.

Fig trees grow 20 to 30 feet high and are typically more broad than tall. They can be considered as tree-like shrubs, or, because they so readily send up new sprouts from ground level, shrub-like trees. Such multi-stemmed fig trees are common in climates where winter cold periodically kills all or portions of the trees to ground level.

Looking below ground, you'd find that, once established, fig roots run deep and wide. (And, also, shallow and wide, as evidenced by the many shallow roots running just below and at the ground surface from the fig trees planted in the ground in my greenhouse.)

In the ground, those far-ranging roots make figs quite drought tolerant; not so, though, for plants growing in the confines of a flower pot or other container.

Above ground, stems can be equally vigorous. Often too much so, with a sacrifice of fruit yield. But that depends, to some degree, on the variety.

A fig tree's *tolerance for abuse* is yet another asset for cold-climate fig growers. The stems are quite flexible and the roots regenerate readily. You can bend stems and lop back roots all with no ill effect, which, you'll soon see, is useful for growing figs in cold climates.

All this is not to say that a fig tree will live through a frigid winter and bear good fruits with any amount of abuse. They do need some care, which is my segue to talk about pruning.

Opposite: This fig tree has managed to grow in a wall!

2

PRUNING: VERY IMPORTANT!

*H*OW A FIG TREE IS PRUNED can determine how it grows, how it bears fruit, even how soon it begins to bear fruit. Most pruning is performed during the dormant season, that is, when the plant is leafless and not growing; some pruning may also be beneficial during the growing season.

Once a plant has grown some stems, two kinds of pruning cuts are possible: Either you lop a stem completely back to its origin, a "thinning cut," or you just shorten that stem to some degree, a "heading cut." A plant responds differently to each kind of cut.

Thinning a stem does nothing more than removing it, so is obviously useful where branches are congested and need elbow room or for getting rid of excess aspiring trunks-to-be if a single-trunked plant is what is wanted.

The effect of a heading cut is to coax buds, especially those near the cut, to sprout into new stems. The more severe the heading cut, the more vigorous the ensuing stem growth and the fewer new stems grow. So, a heading cut is useful where you want more branching on a plant or you want vigorous, new stems to grow. All of which—you'll soon see—will relate closely to your harvest.

Pruning heading vs thinning

Heading

- Plant response is to send up new shoots, especially near the pruning cut
- Less severe pruning makes for more new, but shorter shoots vs more severe makes for fewer but long new shoots

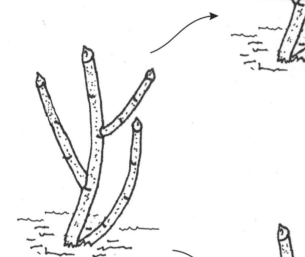

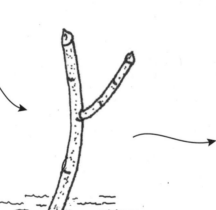

Thinning

- Usually no particular response near the cut
- There is growth, though, not necessarily in response to the thinning

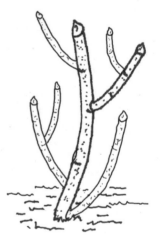

Remember that some fig varieties bear a "main crop" on new, growing stems; some varieties bear a "breba crop" on one-year-old stems; and some varieties bear on both ages of stems, yielding both a "main crop" and a "breba crop." Prune severely if you're going for a main crop only, which is always the case if the particular variety bears only a main crop. Or if you're growing a variety whose main crop tastes better than the breba crop. Or if some practical reason dictates pruning for a main crop only. (I will elaborate on this later.) Drastic pruning removes many, or all, of the year-old stems, but awakens vigorous growth the coming season, vigorous new shoots that will bear figs.

The more severely stems are pruned, the later fruits begin ripening. In regions with shorter or cooler summers, bearing might begin too late for the fruits to ripen following very severe pruning. Here on my farmden (more than a garden, less than a farm), where winters are frigid and summers are hot, but not super-long, I never prune closer than to within a couple of feet of ground level to make sure fruit has time to ripen. I also wouldn't prune too severely if I grew figs where cool summers slowed ripening.

After pruning, your plant could be left with a single, older stem a couple or more feet high. New, fruiting shoots will grow

Pruning for Main Crop Only

Main crop only, "growing season pruning"

Fig before pruning

Severely head back last season's shoots, leave about 2′ old growth

Plant bears on new shoots that grow from the upper part of the plant

Cut all new growth back again to the same point

from this stem, especially near its top. That stem could be permanent, cut back every late fall or winter to regrow shoots each spring that follows. You could leave more than one of these permanent stems; I prefer to leave only one for neatness and to avoid crowding of new shoots.

(Here in Zone 5 I've occasionally heard some gardener bragging about how their figs survived winter outdoors without protection. Yes, the plants can survive frigid temperatures—the roots, that is, especially if the ground is mulched for further insulation. Come spring, new shoots sprout at ground level. The problem is that when cut back that low, whether by winter cold or pruning shears, fruits form late, without enough time to ripen.)

Because the breba crop forms on one-year-old stems, pruning a plant for a breba crop demands more restraint. The goal is to leave enough stems for a good crop earlier in the coming season but also to plan for a future crop. That plan is for next season's breba crop. Cut back some of the stems severely enough to coax

Pruning for Breba Crop Only

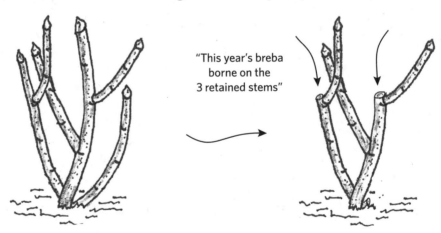

"This year's breba borne on the 3 retained stems"

Fig before pruning

Some heading cuts (shown with arrows) for new shoots for next year's brebas

new growth this coming season for a good supply of breba-bearing, one-year-old stems next season. Leave some other stems full length to bear the coming season's breba crop. The following dormant season, you'll remove those now two-year-old stems unless, of course, you want the plant to grow bigger.

What about the fig variety that bears both a breba and a main crop? In this case, split the difference, removing or shortening more of the one-year-old stems than you would have if you wanted only a breba crop. Again, don't shorten those stems which will bear the coming season's main crop too much or that crop will begin ripening too late in the season.

Pruning isn't only for fruit. You might also need to prune to keep stems from overcrowding. Ridding a plant of excess stems allows those that remain to bask in sunlight and breezes. In fact, this pruning might be almost all that's needed to stimulate growth

Pruning for Both Main Crop and Breba Crop

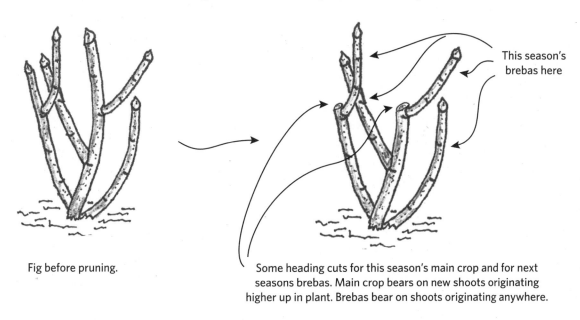

This season's brebas here

Fig before pruning.

Some heading cuts for this season's main crop and for next seasons brebas. Main crop bears on new shoots originating higher up in plant. Brebas bear on shoots originating anywhere.

of new stems for a breba crop the following year. Also prune off any spindly, weak stems as well as stems that are diseased, dead, or rubbing against other stems.

Summer pruning sometimes helps develop or hasten ripening of a main crop. One recommendation is to pinch (remove just the growing point of) a barren stem when it has made 5 to 8 leaves. Another recommendation is to pinch shoots having 2 buds in the juncture where a leaf meets the stem.

How you prune depends on what method of cold-climate growing you choose as well as, of course, the varieties you grow.

3

FIVE METHODS FOR GROWING FIGS IN COLD CLIMATES

BUT FIRST: HOW TO CARE FOR THE SOIL AND NOURISH YOUR FIGS

I CALL TO MIND THOREAU'S ADVICE (in *Walden*) "Simplify, simplify" when it comes to caring for the soil and nourishing plants. This approach can be summed up in two words: "organic matter." Organic matter is a mishmash term for anything that is or was once living. It includes bulky organic materials such as wood chips, manures, compost, straw, leaves, pine needles, grass clippings, hay, and wood shavings, as well as more nutrient-dense organic materials like soybean meal and fish meal.

Organic matter—especially bulky organic materials—benefit soils and plants nutritionally, biologically, and physically. Nutritionally, they offer a wide spectrum of nutrients as well as increased accessibility to nutrients already in the ground. Biologically, they support a population of friendly microorganisms that helps feed plants and fend off pests. And physically, they create a soil structure that supports a good balance of air and water.

Organic matter can fulfill all of your plants' nutritional needs, given a sufficient amount and enough time. The best way to apply any bulky organic material is simple. Merely spread it over the ground as a mulch 2 or 3 inches deep, refreshed as needed so bare soil never peeks through. (A workable metric equivalent would be 5 to 7 cm.)

Bulky organic materials which are from older parts of plants—wood shavings and straw, for example—are low in nutrients, especially nitrogen (but high in valuable carbon). Nitrogen is the nutrient plants need in greatest amount and the one that is most fleeting in the soil. Over time, though, even nutrient-poor, bulky organic materials decompose to build up a reserve of nutrients, including nitrogen, in the soil (as well as provide the above-mentioned benefits).

In a poor soil or where copious amounts of organic matter have not been applied over the years, make up for any nitrogen shortfall with a more concentrated organic source of nitrogen. Some sources and their percentages of nitrogen are:

Alfalfa meal (3%)
Blood meal (13%)
Cottonseed meal (7%)
Feather meal (13%)
Fish meal (13%)
Soybean meal (7%)

Spread any of these nitrogen sources over the surface of the ground at the rate of 0.2 pounds of actual nitrogen per 100 square feet. To compute the amount needed, divide 0.2 by the percent nitrogen in the material (0.07 for 7% for soybean meal), which would call for, as examples, about 3 pounds of soybean meal or 1.5 pounds of feather meal per hundred square feet. (For metric use 100 grams of actual nitrogen per 10 square meters. That would be 1.5 kilograms soybean meal and 750 grams feather meal per 10 square meters.)

Within a container for a potted fig, there's insufficient room for enough of most bulky organic materials to feed the plant on their own. That's why I add soybean meal to my homemade potting mix (recipe below). This is in addition to refreshing a portion of the potting mix with new mix each year or two.

For my figs planted in open ground or in my greenhouse, every year I spread an inch depth of compost (a relatively nutrient-rich, bulky organic material) beneath the plants to feed them. I top the compost with 2 or 3 inches of wood chips, wood shavings, or any other bulky organic material I can get my hands on, mostly to conserve soil moisture and, over time, to decompose and slowly enrich the soil with nutrients. If the figs are growing too rampantly, I'll forgo the compost.

Most important in soil care is to look at your plants. Well-nourished fig plants strut their stuff with good growth and healthy-looking, green leaves (except in autumn when they turn color). But don't be too ready to blame poor growth or off-color leaves on a nutritional problem. Also consider pests or some abiotic problem, such as too much or too little water, or freezing temperatures, as culprits. And finally, guard against overfeeding, especially with nitrogen, which can spur fig plants to overly rampant growth, low productivity, and less flavorful fruits.

In addition to "Simplify, simplify" when it comes to soil care and nourishing my fig plants, I also follow the old adage that, "The best fertilizer is the gardener's shadow."

Method #1:

GROW IN A CONTAINER

Planting

A fig plant can easily be grown in just about any size container, as long as the container has holes in its bottom for drainage of excess water. I grew my first fig, and still grow many figs, in containers. That first one grew in a clay flowerpot about a foot in diameter. (Metric equivalent is about 30 cm.)

Purchase a plant and pot it up using any standard potting mix. Straight garden soil, even good garden soil, is unsuitable for potted plants; it will leave roots gasping for air because of a too high "perched water table," the excess water that unavoidably sits at the bottom of any pot. (Out in the garden, this problem does not arise because of the greater depth of soil.) Some sort of aggregate, such as the perlite, sand, or vermiculite contained in a potting mix, avoids this problem.

Potting mixes for fig plants (and just about any other plant)

These days, commercial potting mixes rarely contain any real soil. Real soil is just too hard to obtain in reliable and uniform quantities for commercial packaging.

Soilless mixes are made from equal parts of organic material and aggregate, with possible additions also of fertilizer, ground limestone, and a wetting agent. Organic materials in these mixes, such as peat moss, coir, or sawdust, help sponge up water and cling to nutrients that might otherwise wash away. Aggregate, such as vermiculite or perlite, is added to soilless mixes to help aerate them, preventing waterlogging by lowering the perched water table in the bottom of the container.

Soilless mixes have advantages beyond their uniformity. They are lightweight and sterile, or easily sterilized, to help avoid problems with soil-borne diseases and weed seeds. You can make up your own soilless potting mix by blending and moistening equal volumes of peat moss and perlite, adding 3 tablespoons of limestone for every 5 gallons of mix. (A workable metric equivalent would be 45 mL of

---

Components of a traditional potting mix

limestone to 20 liters of mix.) Rub the mix through a ½-inch sieve after blending.

Still, problems can arise using soilless mixes. Without the buffering power of real soil, more careful attention is needed to the correct feeding of plants. And feed you must, because the organic materials and aggregates used in soilless mixes have little nutrient value. Also, diseases can arrive from spores that waft through the air, from dirty tools or fingers, or from seeds, cuttings, or plants already carrying diseases. Once diseases get a foothold, they can run amok without having to battle any of the beneficial microorganisms present in real soil.

I prefer a mix containing real soil and compost. This more traditional mix lessens potential nutrient problems and is teeming with beneficial microorganisms. I make up this mix by combining good garden soil with equal parts peat, perlite, and compost.

Thoroughly mixing potting soil components

For every 5 gallons of this mix, I add ¼ cup of limestone and, for long-lasting, slow release of nitrogen (in addition to that provided by the compost), ½ cup of soybean meal. (For metric measure you could use 60 mL of limestone and 120 mL of soybean meal to 20 liters of mix.) For extra good measure and micronutrients, I also occasionally throw in a handful of ground kelp, although it's probably superfluous because of the compost in the mix. I stir the components together with a shovel and then shake them together through ½" mesh hardware cloth.

Shake and rub potting mix through ¼" or ½" mesh

Summer and Winter Lodging

The potted fig spends summers basking in heat and sunlight outdoors. For winter it needs to be moved where it can be protected from bitter cold, ideally to a location where temperatures lie between about 30 to 45°F (-1 to 7° C). But come autumn, don't rush the plant into its winter home. As long as subfreezing temperatures are not predicted, staying outdoors as long as possible lets the stems thoroughly harden off and naturally drop their leaves. I pull off any leaves that don't drop naturally.

Here in Zone 5, my potted trees go into their winter homes around the middle of December. My barely heated basement or, more recently, an insulated, walk-in cooler (which is not just for figs and also has a small electric heater to keep the temperature from falling too low) provide my potted figs with their winter home. An unheated mudroom, foyer, or garage might also provide suitable conditions. No need for light during winter storage, hardly even water. Water just enough to keep the plant from dessicating.

Now for the tricky part: Being subtropical, fig is anxious to grow when in some way—mostly from temperature and soil moisture—it feels winter is ending. Try to keep it asleep with minimal water and cold temperatures as long as possible. Otherwise, the plants tend to awaken before it's warm enough for them to go outside.

In the ideal world, the plant is kept dormant until outdoor temperatures reliably remain in the high 20s (-2 to -3°C), at which point the plant gets moved outdoors, where its leaves unfold naturally in synch with the increasingly warm temperatures of spring.

In the real world, figs sometimes sprout new leaves while still indoors. These new leaves and attendant growth are too succulent to face the great outdoors even when temperatures turn reliably

Potted figs are also ornamental

warm. The overanxious plant will have to be very gradually ac-
climated—hardened off, just like vegetable seedlings—to bright
sunlight, cooler and fluctuating temperatures, and wind. Unless
the prematurely awakened plant can bask in abundant light, as in
a sunroom or greenhouse, its new growth will not likely set fruit,
at least not until it gets moved to better light conditions.

Harden the plant off by initially moving it outside to a spot
with dappled sunlight and shelter from wind. Be ready to whisk
it indoors, temporarily, if very cold or windy weather threatens.
Gradually move the plant to a location with greater and greater
exposure to the elements.

Another option is to just move the plant outdoors to its summer location, and accept a certain amount of die-back. That could
delay or diminish the crop but, except if temperatures turn very
cold, will probably not kill the plant. You also could whisk the
plant through a doorway into your home or garage to provide a
day or two of shelter until outdoor conditions settle again.

Once a plant is outdoors, water regularly, as needed. No
formula here, because "as needed" depends on outdoor temperatures, sunlight, density and composition of the potting soil, and
the size of the plant. The best way to tell if your plant is thirsty
is with an inexpensive, electronic "moisture tester" whose metal
probe you slide deep into the potting soil each time you want to
measure moisture level. Depending on the fertility of your potting mix, water soluble fertilizer, used as per directions, may be
needed. Look at your plant for symptoms of distress from either
hunger, which would cause off-color leaves or weak growth, or
thirst, which would cause wilting leaves. But be aware that diseases might also cause off-color leaves, and too much water or
fertilizer also can result in wilting.

An inexpensive electronic moisture probe easily tells you whether watering is needed

Stem Pruning

What about pruning a container-grow fig? Prune in fall, just before moving the plant to its winter home, or in spring, just before moving the plant outdoors. Two considerations in pruning: First, the bigger the plant, the more stems on which to hang fruit and the bigger the crop; and second, since one-year-old shoots will not be exposed to killing cold, they can be left for a breba crop, assuming the particular variety bears a breba crop.

The other consideration, as I am regularly reminded each time I muscle my potted figs down the narrow, steep stairs to my basement each fall and back up each spring, is that the bigger the plant and pot, the heavier and more unwieldy it is to move. So I prune my potted figs in fall, before I move them to their winter homes. In contrast, an 89-year-old neighbor (Italian, of course) is able to easily move her many fig trees, growing in four-foot-diameter pots, into and out of winter storage because the pots are on wheels and the storage area is part of a paved area near where the plants summer outdoors.

If you can manage moving the plant indoors and outdoors with the seasons, leave some stems on a variety that produces a breba crop, for the upcoming season's brebas, and shorten some stems to coax new growth for the upcoming season's main crop. You gotta do what you gotta do.

Shorten all stems for a main-crop-only variety, but not too much or the crop will begin forming too late to ripen. As I wrote previously, leaving a couple of feet of old wood from which to sprout new shoots is about right.

If, after being pruned, stems spread too wide, I bend and tie them together to make the plant easier to wend through doorways as it's being moved.

Maria and Giuseppi and their potted fig orchard

Branches pruned and tied together readies plant for winter storage

Root Pruning

Eventually, roots are going to fill any container, leaving no room for new root growth; and the plant will have gobbled up all the nutrients in the potting mix. If the plant is destined for a larger container, repot it. Roots will grow and enjoy the new space and soil.

If the plant is already in a pot that is its permanent home, make space for new soil with root pruning. That is, slice off some roots to make space for new soil in the same pot. Trust me—I've done this for many years and although the operation looks brutal, the plants tolerate it well, growing happily each spring following the operation. Fall or spring, when the plants are leafless, is the best time for root pruning and repotting.

To root prune, I tip the plant on its side and pull on the stem while holding the pot in place so the root ball can be easily slid out of the pot. After standing the root ball upright, I start slicing the root ball from top to bottom. For root balls 18 to 24 inches across, slicing a couple inches off all around is about right. The old kitchen knife that I once used has been replaced by a reciprocating saw with a medium-tooth blade, which works much better.

Root pruning

Repotting fig

With the root ball shrunken, back it goes into its pot with fresh potting soil filling in the space around the sides of the pot. For good contact, I pack the potting soil in with my fingers and the flat end of a ¾-inch dowel.

For very large containers, no need to actually remove the root ball. Just cut straight down and across to remove segments of the root ball, perhaps from one side one year and the other side the next time the plant is root pruned. Then pack soil into the space that remains after you lift segments up and out of the pot.

The following year or, at least every two years, trees should get root-pruned again.

A healthy fig tree grows rapidly. Eventually its trunk will expand to a diameter too wide for a pot. What to do then? Figs are easy to root from cuttings: Take a cutting before the trunk grows too large in order to have a new, fruiting plant ready. Or cut the whole plant back and select a new trunk from a root sprout. Or cut back the plant and, with a saw, cut vertically down into the root crown of the plant to divide it into two or more new plants. Pot each one up separately; at least one will probably survive to make a new plant.

PROS OF METHOD #1

- Decorative potted plant in summer.
- Potential for breba and/or main crop (depending on variety).
- Very reliable way to get fruit.

CONS OF METHOD #1

- Careful attention needed to watering in summer.
- Suitable place for winter lodging required.
- Timing is important for moving the plant outdoors in spring.
- Plant and, hence crop, size limited by size of pot that can be managed.
- Root pruning needed every year or two.

Method #2:

PLANT IN GROUND EACH SPRING, DIG UP EACH FALL

Planting

With this method, plant your fig right in the ground in a suitable location. That is, at a site bathed in sunlight in well-drained soil of moderate fertility.

If the season is fall or winter, and the weather is too cold for your new fig plant to be outdoors, either store it with its roots kept moist—in moist potting soil wrapped in plastic—or else pot it up. Keep the plant cool to hold back growth until outdoor planting time. If dormant and small enough, the plant can count a refrigerator as its temporary home. Plant the fig outdoors once warm weather settles in.

The ideal is to get good growth this first season. If it's good enough, and the particular variety is one that bears main crop figs, you might get to pick ripe fruit this first season. Good growth is achieved with adequate fertility, which might be provided by nothing more than a one-inch depth mulch of compost around the plant, and water, as needed.

At the end of the season, weather that has turned consistently cold, with night temperatures regularly dipping into the 20s, signals that it's time to dig the plant up to bring it to a protected location. (Another signal would be the ground freezing about an inch deep.) How big a root ball to take up with the plant depends in large part on your physical ability to maneuver the plant and root ball to winter quarters. You can lighten the load by shaking off some excess soil from the outside portions of the root ball. Not too much though.

Pruning back stems also lightens your load, and makes it easier to bring the plant to its winter quarters. For ease of moving, I would suggest growing a variety that bears a main crop so that the plant can be pruned severely at the end of each season.

Again, not too severely; leave at least 2 to 3 feet of old stem to allow for timely ripening the following growing season.

With stems pruned and the plant out of the ground, sprinkle some water on the roots and then put the root portion of the plant into a plastic bag tied shut around the stem or stems. Alternatively, put the root portion of the plant into any container having drainage holes and pack autumn leaves, wood shavings, wood chips, or other loose, absorbent organic material into the space between the wall of the container and the root ball. Sprinkle water on the pot. Roots should not dry out. Wrapped in a plastic bag, my plants usually go all winter without further water. In a container, where the top layer of soil is open to air, occasional watering might be needed depending on the humidity and temperature of storage location.

Options for winter storage and removal from winter storage are the same as for Method #1 (see above).

Come late winter or spring, I just drop the root ball into a waiting hole and give the plant a thorough watering.

Fig stored through winter in cool basement with roots wrapped to keep them moist

Replanting root ball in
spring

Water replanted fig
thoroughly after planting

A Variation

One season I came up with a way to avoid guesstimating how big a hole to dig to excise the root ball from the ground and make excision easier. I drilled a number of holes (½" diameter, but the diameter is not critical) into the side, including near the bottom, of a large, black plastic flower pot (about 18" in diameter, but also not critical). Into this pot went a fig plant along with potting soil.

For its first season, the plant was treated just like any container-grown fig, with plenty of sunlight and regular watering, followed by—at season's end—winter storage at a cool location.

When winter's coldest cold had passed, in a sunny spot with well-drained soil, I dug a hole in the ground just large enough to plant the pot with the fig. Regular watering of the pot and surrounding soil for the first couple of weeks got the plant off to a good start.

First season of growth for the potted fig in the ground

As the plant grew, its roots reached out beyond the confines of the container into surrounding soil to eventually make the plant more independent and larger than if it had been confined to the container.

Growth at the end of first season, for the potted fig in the ground

At season's end, I dug up the pot by slicing off all roots growing out the holes with a shovel or pruning shears. Since all those roots were just one season old, none were unduly thick, making cutting easy.

A healthy fig's trunk will rapidly thicken until, at some point, the plant may be unwieldy and heavy to move in and out of its winter quarters. Deal with this situation the same way as I described for Method #1.

Roots grow out hole each season for potted fig in ground

PROS OF METHOD #2

- Best for varieties that bear a good main crop.
- Plant is self-sufficient in summer.
- Bigger plant and, hence, bigger crop than with Method #1.

CONS OF METHOD #2

- Suitable place for winter lodging required.
- Timing is important for moving the plant outdoors in spring.

Growth at end of second
season for the potted fig
in the ground

Method #3:

SWADDLE STEMS

Swaddling stems is a method that will get you figs, most years, in Cold Hardiness Zones 6 and warmer. The idea here is to wrap the stems of an outdoor planted fig to fend off the harshest bite of winter cold. Such "sculptures" often grace the front or back-yards of gardeners, especially those with genealogical roots in the Mediterranean.

As with the other methods, plants should be allowed to experience some cold weather before being swaddled. This experience toughens them for deeper cold. Also, wrapping stems while the weather is still warm would invite rot and rodents.

Once temperatures have dropped reliably, but not below the low 20s, a number of materials can be used to fend off colder weather. Tying the stems together into a tight bundle facilitates wrapping. What to use depends on what's available and the degree of cold expected. Burlap suffices in regions where temperatures hardly dip below the 'teens (-10 to -13°C). Colder than that, and blankets or, for even more cold protection, some sort of insulating material can be used.

Rain must be kept off the top of the fig "sculpture." An upside-down bucket capping the bound together and wrapped stems could complete the picture.

Even though winter lows here on my farmden dip in some years to minus 20°F (-29°C) or lower, I tried the swaddling method on a fig planted in the ground near the south-facing brick wall of my home. The wall would absorb some solar heat and re-radiate it towards the plant. Or so I hoped. I erected a temporary enclosure, a circle about 4-feet in diameter, with stakes and a 4-foot-high plastic fence. Wood shavings filled this enclosure, which was then capped with a circle of plastic.

My swaddling attempt was a failure. The fig died to ground level and the vigorous, new shoots that sprouted did not have time to ripen their crop.

The point is that wrapping stems provides only a few degrees of increased cold resistance.

Pruning

Avoid training the plant to a single, permanent trunk because it might suffer cold damage and die back to the ground some years. More than one trunk provides insurance. Use moderate pruning, involving mostly thinning cuts. These cuts remove enough stems (which might go on to become trunks) so they do not crowd.

Cut back the plant, as needed, to fit into its swaddling. For a breba crop, make sure to leave some 1-year-old stems. For a main crop, avoid shortening the plant too much or else that crop will begin ripening later, perhaps too late.

A fig tree wrapped and capped to survive winter cold

After standing through winter waterproofed and swaddled in insulation, a fig tree is being unwrapped in the spring.

PROS OF METHOD #3

· Plant is self-sufficient in summer.
· Breba crop, main crop, or both are possible, depending on the variety's bearing habit.

CONS OF METHOD #3

· Not a viable method in colder winter climates (colder than Zone 6).
· Plant might be considered either an eyesore or... well... a "sculpture" in its winter swaddling, depending on your aesthetic, swaddling materials, and capping "hat."

Method #4:

LAY DOWN OR BURY STEMS

Okay, here's a method of growing figs outdoors that will have you harvesting fresh figs no matter how cold your winter lows are. It's based on the fact that the ground is a repository of heat. Dig a few feet into the ground and the temperature is always balmy, around 50°F.

Laying fig stems down on the ground and then covering them with some sort of insulating material keeps them warmer than if they were upright, even upright and wrapped with some sort of insulating material. Even more cold protection can be had by digging a trench in which to lay down the stems and then covering the trench. Whether to lay down or bury stems, and how deeply to bury them, and how much to cover them depends on the degree of winter cold expected.

As I wrote early on, "the fig is an adaptable plant," both above ground and below ground. When I lived in Wisconsin, a local Italian food store was home to two large fig trees, trees that survived outdoors with trunks a few inches in diameter despite temperatures reliably dropping below minus 25°F (-32°C) each winter! These trees were planted in the bottom of 4-foot-deep trenches into which the trunks were gradually lowered late each autumn. (More on this below.) Once the trees were down, old

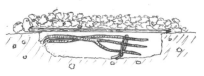

Bending fig tree down for covering from winter cold

Nothing new

Over a hundred years ago, James Worthington wrote of bending down and burying fig stems to protect them from cold. His success was attributed to planting on mounds or ridges, for drainage, and then, in autumn, burying stems beneath 3 to 4 inches of soil topped with a couple of inches of mulch. The stems were disinterred around corn planting time. (To me, it seems that he buried them a bit too early and, phenologically speaking, disinterred them a bit too late.)

Similarly, fig branches were interred for winter outside Paris over a hundred years ago, and, once disinterred, pruned rather elaborately. (There, the problem was not winter cold but lack of summer heat. The reason for burying the branches was to delay growth as protection against spring frosts, which evidently were common there then.) Weak branches were removed, strong branches shortened to two to three buds, and fruiting branches had their leaf buds removed, except for a couple of them near the base of the branch, a couple along the stem, and the one growing from the terminal bud. But there's more to it, which you can find in Gustave Eisen's book referenced in the appendix.

doors were laid over the trenches topped by piles of autumn leaves. Through winter, temperatures in that trench remained cool, but not frigid. Come spring, a system of pulleys gradually lifted the trunks to a vertical orientation. The plants bore heavily, with fresh, ripe figs that sold well.

Pruning

If only moderate protection from cold is needed, prune the plant each fall to have 3 or 4 one-year-old stems. These stems could bear a breba crop; later on, a main crop could be borne on new shoots growing off those stems. Reducing the plant each year to just a few young stems makes it easier to bend them down each autumn.

Older wood, or even a trunk, could be developed but would require a larger trench or more insulation for protection, as well as more effort to get the plant down in autumn and up in spring.

With branches tied and roots cut, a fig is ready to lower into the ground for winter. Photo credit: Marry Menniti

Fig wood is flexible, but the plant is even easier to lay prone if a shovel is driven into the ground to sever roots on the side opposite the direction it's going to be pushed down. Or, in a trench the fig could be planted at a 45 degree angle so that the stem needs to flex less when being bent down or being resurrected.

Insulate

Once the plant is down, pile leaves, wood shavings, wood chips, or other insulating material atop the stems—with more depth the greater the degree of cold expected—to create a cozy, warm environment. If a greater degree of cold protection is required, dig a shallow trench in which to bury the stems. Or, if even more protection is required, dig a deeper trench à la Madison, Wisconsin Italian food store method that I mentioned above.

Ground level or below, stems covered with insulating material would be subject to rot; avoid this with a final cover of plastic or tar paper to keep out moisture. That could be covered with more insulating material, for greater cold protection and/or for decoration. (To me, the covered fig plants are not all that attractive a sight in winter; the look is that of a burial ground.)

A fig bent down to or below ground level provides both food (fig stems) and cozy lodging for rodents in winter. Be inhospitable. Wait as long as possible to lay your plant down and cover it, by which time rodents will, hopefully, have found other lodging. Paint or spray stems with a homemade or commercial rodent repellent; typical ingredients might include hot pepper, castor oil, peppermint, predatory animal urine and/or Thiram (a fungicide with a strong sulfur aroma). Or set traps and/or utilize the services of a good cat.

Uncover

As with the previously mentioned methods, the ideal situation is for the plant to be still dormant when exposed—in this case, by

stems having their cover removed and lifted upright—to the great outdoors in late winter or early spring. Then late freezes won't threaten the plant's health. The fully dormant stems are good to about 20°F (-7°C) or lower, but its cold tolerance decreases as it comes increasingly awake in spring.

This fig laid in the ground and ready to be covered for winter.

PHOTO CREDIT: MARRY MENNITI

PROS OF METHOD #4

- Large crops possible.
- Breba and main crop possible.
- Self-sufficient during growing season.

CONS OF METHOD #4

- Mice and rabbit damage possible in winter; avoid with repellants, traps, and/or cats.
- Timing is important for when to lay down or bury and cover a plant.
- Possibly not very attractive in winter.

Method #5:

IN GROUND, IN COOL OR UNHEATED GREENHOUSE OR HOOP HOUSE

Method #5 is my favorite method for growing figs in cold climates, primarily because of the large and early crops possible. Of course, it does require a greenhouse or a hoop house. (A hoop house is a more primitive greenhouse, usually with plants growing directly in the ground, and unheated, except by sunlight, and with a single cover of clear plastic film.)

Planting is simple in a greenhouse or hoop house. Just dig a hole and plant, just as you would outdoors with any other tree or shrub. Ideally, the floor of the greenhouse is dirt, not concrete. Alternatively, the plant could be grown in a large (or small) pot, but that doesn't optimize the use of the greenhouse for growing figs; plant size will be limited and the plant will require root pruning and repotting as well as more frequent watering.

Commercial potential for hoop house or greenhouse figs

Blanketing fig trees with an additional layer of protection in a minimally heated or unheated greenhouse or hoop house has potential for growing figs for market. Winter salad greens are often grown in such structures, and the fig trees would not at all mind the cold temperatures in which these greens thrive. Being leafless and pruned, severely if grown for their main crop only, the fig trees also would not shade the winter crops.

The kind of covering—the blanket—needed to protect the plants depends on the degree of outdoor cold and whether or not the structure is heated. Minimal protection, a few degrees, is afforded by "floating row covers" ("fleece" in Britain), which are spun fabrics that admit light and water. More cold protection would come from a cloth or insulated fabric cover. An incandescent light bulb beneath the blanket would offer even more protection for a particularly cold night in an unheated hoop house or greenhouse.

Depending on the depth of winter cold and the size of the hoop house or greenhouse, extra heat may or may not be needed. The smaller the structure, the unavoidably closer the plants are to an outside wall and cold. Another option for getting fruit with little or no added heat would be to train plants low so that stems could be covered with blankets or something else to add another layer of cold protection.

Jonathan's Figloo

Jonathan Bates (www.foodforestfarm.com) is a fig enthusiast who manages to harvest fresh figs in his unheated hoop house in Cold Hardiness Zone 6. His approach is to bend or train branches just above ground level and then "put them to bed" in autumn in an enclosure of straw bales one bale high. Over the bales go a roof of rigid foam insulation. The young trees have already borne well.

Straw bales and cozy warmth are a recipe for vole heaven. Including food, in the form of fig stems in winter and fruit in summer. Jonathan keeps voles at bay with the help of cats, by trapping, and by painting fig stems with a mix of lime whitewash and oil impregnated with hot pepper and garlic.

Problems have been late frost damage in spring and the need to bag fruits to thwart sowbugs.

Greenhouse economics

Having a heated greenhouse in which to grow fig trees need not be an extravagance. My greenhouse is minimally heated, just enough to keep temperatures from dropping below about 35°F. The greenhouse is also a winter home to lettuce, mâche, celery, kale, chard, and other plants that thrive under the cool, short-day conditions of that season in the greenhouse. Shade from the fig plants is not an issue because the plants are dormant, mostly cut back, and leafless all winter; the winter rest is also to the fig's liking. And finally, shelves in the greenhouse provide space for raising all the vegetable and flower seedlings for each season's garden. Along with the figs, in summer, I grow ginger, and sometimes cucumbers, in the beds. All that's a lot of bang for the buck.

Water

In-ground plants in a greenhouse or hoop house may or may not need supplemental watering. In my greenhouse, roots of plants near side or end walls creep underneath the walls to drink up rainwater that falls outside the greenhouse. Even plants growing near the middle of the greenhouse seem to get by with little or no water in summer, testimonial to a fig tree's far-reaching roots and/or the shallow depth of my water table.

Crops I grow on the ground beneath the fig plants get irrigated regularly and automatically (via drip irrigation). Figs also drink in that water from autumn until spring, when ground level crops are being irrigated in my minimally heated greenhouse.

Pruning

The usual problem with greenhouse figs is that the plants grow very rapidly and get out of hand to eventually create a self-shading jungle with few figs for the size of the plant, and many of those out of easy reach. In the past, my approach was to prune severely in late autumn, leaving just a few full-length stems on those varieties that bear breba crops. Through the growing season I would periodically shorten or lop back branches that were tickling the greenhouse roof, were figless, or crowding each other.

A few years ago I decided to organize my greenhouse figs more rigorously by training the figs as espaliers, which is an ancient method of training plants to two-dimensional patterns that are decorative, formal, and, for fruits, very productive. The result has been quicker pruning, better air circulation, and more light on the branches.

Along the back wall of my greenhouse, I trained one fig plant to the shape of a low branching T. Training began right after planting, when I removed all but one vertical stem. When the stem, which I will now call a "trunk," reached about 18" in height I pruned off the tip, which caused buds just below the cut to grow

Mature double cordon espalier; note crop

out into shoots. I selected two, on opposite sides of the trunk, and trained them (they are now called "cordons") in opposite directions along a temporarily mounted, horizontal bamboo cane.

Figs planted at the heads of each of the greenhouse beds were trained similarly, minus one of the cordons of the T. With two opposing cordons, like the back wall fig, the plants would have blocked the main path of the greenhouse which runs perpendicular to the beds.

In early spring, new shoots appear. The goal is upright shoots originating about 8" apart along the cordons; to that end I prune away any shoots that are growing downwards or crowd closer than 8" from a neighbor. To keep everything neat and orderly I attached thin bamboo canes to the greenhouse roof to reach down to the cordons, one cane at each location of an upright. Each cane provides an anchor for each upwardly mobile, new fig shoot.

Single cordon espaliers at head of each greenhouse bed

Shoots eventually grow roof-height so I cut back the tops a bit, as needed, and shorten side branches that then develop near that growing tip. The same goes for other side branches that might develop lower down along the growing shoots.

Major pruning takes place at season's end, and it's very easy. In addition to cutting back any root sprouts or new shoots developing along the trunk, I cut every vertical shoot down to the cordon from which it sprang. And once a cordon has grown the desired length, I cut all new growth from its tip back to its origin for that season. That's it! Because of the retained length of trunk and cordon, new shoots begin growth earlier than if the plant had been cut back more severely, and ripening of the main crop begins earlier.

Pruned single cordon espalier at head of greenhouse beds

PROS OF METHOD #5

- Fruit is not accessible to birds and bees, wasps, and yellow jackets.
- Large main crops possible.
- Self-sufficient during growing season
- Can be integrated as money crop into a greenhouse or hoop house along with other crops.
- Very easy to prune.
- Air and light thoroughly bathe all the stems and fruits.

CONS OF METHOD #5

- Greenhouse or hoop house needed, possibly with supplemental heat.

4

WHAT KIND OF COLD DO YOU HAVE?

IG TREES GROW AND THRIVE in many climates that are much colder than the Arabian courtyard we imagined early on. There's no doubt that too much winter cold will kill fig stems or that lack of summer heat can unduly delay fruit ripening. Yet none of this obviates growing figs in most cold climates; it merely speaks to the question of which method or methods of cold-climate growing to choose from, and which varieties to grow.

"Cold" climates can differ from each other in a few ways.

Fig Region 1

Let's call "frigid" any place where the average minimum temperature dips below 15°F (-9°C) in winter. At around that temperature, cold kills fig stems. This region also has hot summers, even if they are not particularly long. Fig Region 1 would characterize the climate here on my farmden in New York's Hudson Valley (the temperature is 85°F here, about 30°C, as I write in late June), as well as the climate found over much of the northern portions of continental North America and eastern Europe.

PHOTO CREDIT: JAIME CULPEPPER

65

Fig Region 2

This region is characterized by "frigid" winters and cool summers. Coastal regions of eastern North America get a moderating effect from proximity to the Atlantic Ocean. But go far enough north along the coast, and winter temperatures still drop below 15°F, while that proximity to water keeps summers relatively cool. These conditions are also typical of northern mountain regions throughout the northern hemisphere. Fig Region 2 is the most challenging region in which to raise figs, challenging but still possible.

Fig Region 3

Here, ocean-warmed air currents modify the climate year 'round so that summers are cool (by my standards) but winters are what we can call "coldish," that is, in most years minimum winter temperatures stay above our fig-critical 15°F (-9°C). This region—with coldish winters and cool summers—would include the Pacific Northwest of North America, and England and other parts of northwestern Europe.

So, there you have it, three cold-climate Fig Regions:

Region 1: Frigid winters, hot summers
Region 2: Frigid winters, cool summers
Region 3: Coldish winters, cool summers

What about regions with coldish winters and hot summers. There, just plant figs outdoors in the ground and reap your rewards. That's not "cold-climate fig growing." You'll need to look at a different book.

Information about the average minimum temperatures for given regions often surprises people in that region. They generally assume temperatures don't ever get as cold as reality. My neighbor's eyebrows rose in disbelief when I told him that my thermometers—of which I have multiple: electronic, mercury, and alcohol—read minus 20°F one winter; most winters, in fact. But

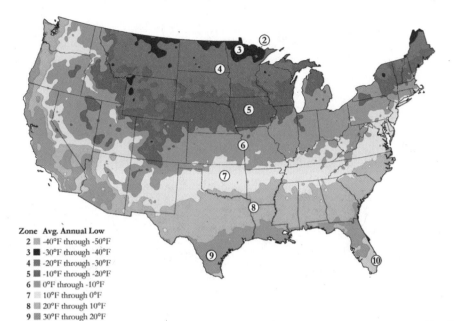

Zone	Avg. Annual Low
2	-40°F through -50°F
3	-30°F through -40°F
4	-20°F through -30°F
5	-10°F through -20°F
6	0°F through -10°F
7	10°F through 0°F
8	20°F through 10°F
9	30°F through 20°F
10	40°F through 30°F

Hardiness zones map for the US, Alaska, and Hawaii. Go to arborday.org to find the zone for your zip code. You can also find trees for planting in your zip code. © 2006 by The National Arbor Day Foundation

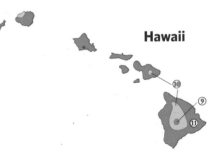

Zone	Avg. Annual Low
1	Below -50°F
2	-40°F through -50°F
3	-30°F through -40°F
4	-20°F through -30°F
5	-10°F through -20°F
6	0°F through -10°F
7	10°F through 0°F
8	20°F through 10°F
9	30°F through 20°F
10	40°F through 30°F
11	Above 40°F

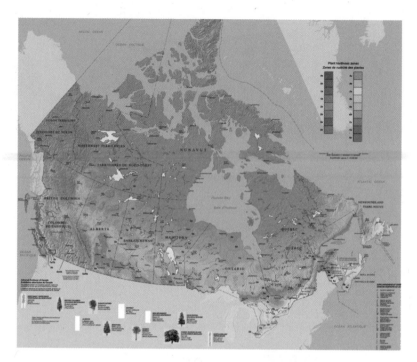

Plant hardiness zones map
for Canada

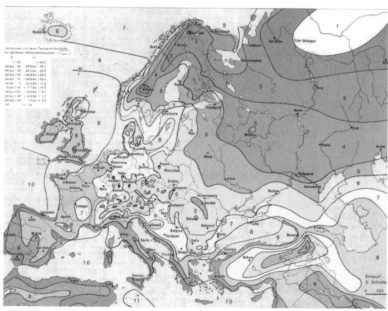

Plant hardiness zones map
for Europe

he didn't have to take my word for it. This information has been recorded and tabulated into the form of a map, a Cold Hardiness Zone map overrun by squiggly lines enclosing colored areas of similar average winter lows, with a number designating that region. Which puts me in Zone 5, with average minimums between -10°F (-23°C) and -20°F (-29°C).

A similar map has been drawn up for Heat Zones, in this case delineating regions by average number of days with temperatures above 86°F (30°C), which is taken to be the temperature at which plants generally begin to suffer damage from heat. (Even figs!?) It's probably a safe assumption that regions with more days above that critical temperature would have warmer summers.

Ah, if only plants were so simple… An absolute cold temperature just doesn't tell the whole story. When cold arrives, and how much cold, is also important. An early, hard freeze in fall can catch plants off guard, before they have hardened off for winter weather. A late freeze in spring as a plant is awakening can nip back expanding buds or tender, new growth; the plant may rebound

At Brooklyn Botanic Garden, the Herb Garden's fig trees (*Ficus carica*) will stay warm for the winter inside their burlap wrapping. Photo by Blanca Begert. Courtesy Brooklyn Botanic Garden.

with newer growth or, depending on timing and depth of cold, be killed back to some degree, even to ground level.

Rainfall can also figure into the mix. Drier weather going into winter helps toughen plants up for the cold weather ahead, but weather that is too dry weakens a plant. Weather or climates that promote active growing well into fall leave plants unprepared for cold weather lying ahead.

DO SOMETHING!

No need to bemoan the less-than-perfect fig weather, wherever you are. In addition to the various techniques for handling your fig plants, you can actually do something about your weather, by paying attention to "microclimates."

Microclimates refer to pockets of weather variation—differences in temperature, humidity, and wind—that exist over even small areas. For instance, a slightly south-facing slope is generally (in the northern hemisphere) warmer than a north-facing one because of being struck more head-on by sunlight.

Also, cold air is heavier than warmer air, and on clear, windless nights, a layer of colder air develops as heat is re-radiated skyward. That cold air, being heavier than warm air, runs downhill like water to settle and build up in low lying areas (like my farmden!). Better to plant up on slopes and let cold air trickle down past.

Shelter from wind creates a microclimate. Especially if that shelter is a masonry wall, which will absorb heat during the day to warm nearby air as it re-radiates that heat by night. In northern Europe, the extra heat needed to ripen figs and peaches was often provided by planting them near south-facing walls, which was the practical origin of espalier.

Microclimate During Day

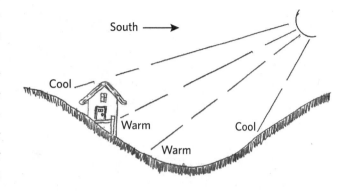

Microclimate During Night

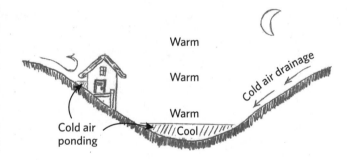

Some fig varieties

5

SOME VARIETIES FOR
COLD CLIMATES?

ORTING OUT FIG VARIETIES is a mess, which is understandable for a plant that's been cultivated for millennia, sprouts readily from viable seeds, has been transported far and wide and then passed on from gardener to gardener, and which can be adapted to many regions beyond its native home. For instance, the variety Brown Turkey has also paraded under such names as Blue Burgundy, Brown Naples, Murrey, and Lee's Perpetual. Further muddying the waters, the name Brown Turkey is also that of a very different variety in California, and this California variety, wrote Gustav Eisen in his 1901 publication for the USDA, is generally "known elsewhere in America as the Brunswick" and is also known as Brown Hamburgh, Madonna, Large White Turkey, and Bayswater. Whew!

So here I sit, about to suggest varieties for growing in cold regions. That's a tall order, one for which I'm drawing on information from government and university sources, amateur growers, and my personal experiences. Cold tolerance is not a simple matter because it's also influenced by a plant's physiological state, perhaps its age, how the cold develops (rapidly or slowly, for example), plant nutrition, and soil moisture preceding and during the cold period.

Look at the leaves

Leaves of fig trees are variable in shape, and that variability is sometimes helpful in correctly identifying a variety. To that end, I have included below some descriptions of leaf shapes characteristic of specific varieties; and here are what they mean.

Of course, there are a limited number of leaf shapes and myriad fig varieties. And, again further muddying the waters: Leaf shapes on an individual variety can be somewhat variable!

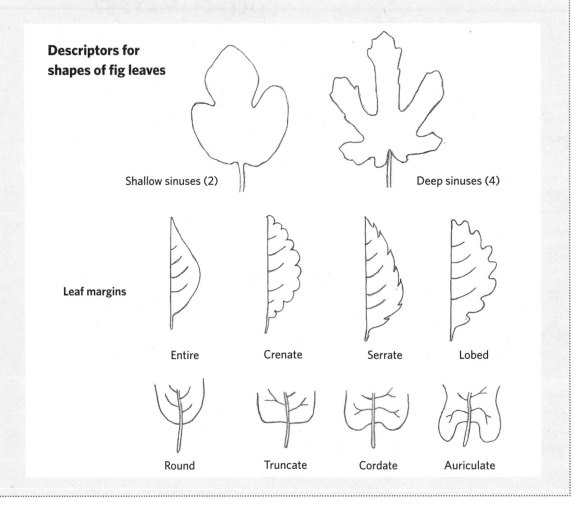

Descriptors for shapes of fig leaves

Shallow sinuses (2)

Deep sinuses (4)

Leaf margins

Entire

Crenate

Serrate

Lobed

Round

Truncate

Cordate

Auriculate

With those caveats, fig varieties most suitable for cold climates would be those that set good breba crops and/or main crops that ripen relatively early in the season, perhaps are able to ripen to good quality even where summers remain relatively cool, and perhaps are also more tolerant of lower temperatures than most varieties. (All those "perhaps" come about because what's needed is also dependent on which of the methods mentioned is used for growing the figs.)

And, of course, taste good. Summer climate has some effect here, as do personal preferences.

Consider this list, then, a sampling of varieties worth a try in cold climates. Figs bear quickly so it doesn't take long to engage in a certain amount of trial and error to find varieties best suited to your climate and growing techniques.

Adriatic (Fragola, Strawberry Fig, Verdone, White Adriatic, Grosse Verte)

- Small to medium-size fruit with greenish skin and strawberry-colored flesh. Rich, mild berry flavor. Good dried or fresh. Little or no breba crop.
- Leaves medium size, glossy above, stiff in texture, and mostly 5 lobed. Upper sinuses are deep and moderately broad; lower sinuses are fairly shallow. Base is broadly subcordate to truncate. Middle lobe is broad at the tip and tapered towards its base, with upper margins coarsely crenate, lower margins entire.
- Large vigorous tree leafs out early so is subject to frost damage. Prune to force new growth. Subject to mosaic disease and, because of its open eye, spoilage organisms. Well-adapted to cool summers.

Alma

- Small to medium-size fruit with golden-brown skin and amber flesh. Sweet and delicate, caramel flavor. Little or no breba crop.

Alma

Black Mission

Brown Turkey

- Leaves are elongated, mostly without, or with very shallow, sinuses, and crenate edges.
- Very productive, compact tree is cold hardy and has a prolonged spring dormancy. Wood is very hardy, but the fruit buds are damaged by hard freezes; especially frost sensitive when young. Comes into production at a very early age. Highly resistant to fruit rot because of eye sealed with a drop of thick resin. An interspecies cross between *F. palmata* and *F. carica*.

Black Mission (Beers Black, Franciscan, Mission)

- Fruits are dark purple and elongated with water-melon-colored flesh. Brebas are prolific, fairly rich, medium to large and pear-shaped. Main crop fruit is medium size. Rich, berry-like flavor.
- Leaves are large, averaging 7 5/8 inches broad and 8 inches in length (19.4 and 20.3 cm). Lobes mostly 5, but sometimes 3, or on vigorous wood with each basal lobe auricled. Upper surface somewhat glossy.
- Tree is very large. Well-adapted to cool summers.

Brown Turkey (Eastern Brown Turkey, English Brown Turkey, Everbearing, La Perpetuelle, Lee's Perpetual, Texas Everbearing)

- Medium size fruit with coppery-brown skin and light strawberry flesh. Sometimes bears both breba and main crop, more often only main crop.
- Leaves are large with lobes having rounded tips; usually about 5 lobes.
- Tree is hardy and productive. Well-adapted to cool summers

Celeste (Blue Celeste, Honey Fig, Malta, Sugar, Violette)

- Small to medium size fruit with light violet to violet-brown skin and reddish amber flesh. Very sweet, caramel flavor. Light breba crop. Tightly closed eye.
- Leaves are small to medium size, glossy, with 3 to 5 lobes. Upper sinuses are moderately deep and broad; lower sinuses are shallow. Leaf base is subcordate. Margins are crenate.
- Small to medium size tree that is very cold hardy and widely adapted. Dense with leaves. Early ripening. Sensitive to excess or deficiency of soil moisture, resulting in fruit drop.

Celeste

Chicago Hardy (St. Rita, Mongibello, Danny's Delight)

- Figs are medium size with distinct necks. Fruit stalk long, about one third the length of the fruit. Distinct ribbing of fruit. Purplish-brown skin and strawberry-pink pulp. Early main crop. Small eye.
- Leaves are medium size with rounded lobes.
- Very hardy. Good for colder winter climates.

Chicago Hardy

Desert King (Charlie, King)

- San Pedro type. Large fruit with deep green skin, minutely spotted white. Strawberry-red flesh. Sweet and rich, delicious fresh or dried. Large breba crop. Sometimes sets a main crop without pollination.
- Leaves medium size, 3 to 5 lobed with subcordate base and broad, shallow sinuses. Margins are shallowly crenate. Upper leaf surface somewhat glossy and rugose.
- Tree is highly vigorous, fairly hardy, and adapted to cool summer areas.

Desert King

Excel

Excel

- Main crop bears yellow fruits with pink flesh. Very sweet. Light breba crop. Very resistant to splitting. Good for canning, drying, and eating fresh.
- Leaves medium size, 5 lobed with fairly deep sinuses. Base is cordate.
- Vigorously growing tree. Very hardy. Fruit resists souring by forming "honey drop" that plugs basal opening. Similar to Kadota but more productive, not quite as tasty, and with a softer skin.

Genoa (White Genoa)

- Medium size fruit with greenish-yellow to white skin and yellow-amber flesh. Good fresh or dried. Light breba and main crops.
- Leaves medium to large size and 3 to 5 lobed with dull upper surface. Upper sinuses are medium depth and width; lower sinuses shallow and broad. Base is broadly subcordate, sometimes auricled. Margins are shallowly crenate.
- Tree upright. Best adapted to cool summer regions. Very late, continuing to ripen even after first frosts.

Improved Celeste

- Small, light brown or violet fruits with pink centers. Light breba crop followed by early ripening main crop.
- Leaves with 1 to 3 lobes.
- Bred from Celeste for less fruit drop, longer harvest, and improved hardiness.

Kadota (Dottato)

- Breba crop heaviest in climates offering warm day and night temperatures in spring. Pale green or yellow fruit with light colored interior. Excellent flavor that is rich and sweet. One of my favorite varieties. The thick skin has a rubbery texture making, for me, the fruit pleasantly chewy.
- Leaves are variable, some unlobed and others with either 3 or 5 lobes. Upper and lower sinuses are shallow. Leaf margins are serrate to coarsely crenate.
- Often pruned heavily for large main crop only. A very ancient variety, highly praised by Roman writer Pliny the Younger in the first century C.E.

Kadota

Lattarula (Italian Honey, Peter's Honey, Blanche Royale, Lemon, Marseilles, Blanche, White Marseilles)

- Medium to large, yellowish-green fruit and very sweet, amber flesh. Productive breba and main crops.
- Leaves medium size, 3 to 5 lobed with glossy upper surface. Upper sinuses have medium depth and are narrow. Lower sinuses are shallow. Base is sub-cordate, sometimes auricled. Margins are crenate. Mature blades often have dead spots.
- Good for cool or warm summer climates. Compact tree.

LSU Purple

- Small to medium size purple fruits with strawberry-colored flesh. Small eye makes it resistant to spoilage. A few brebas in some years. Main crop ripens early.
- Leaves 5 lobed with deep sinuses, cordate base, and wavy edges.

LSU Purple

Violette de Bordeaux

Osborn's Prolific

- Tree is vigorous and cold-tolerant. Good for short season and cool summer climates. Purple stems. Very productive.

Negronne (Bordeaux, Violette de Bordeaux, Figue de Marseille)

- Fruits are medium size, black, with dense red flesh. Breba and main crop.
- Leaves 3 to 5 lobed, deep sinuses, with glossy surface. Leaf base truncate to shallowly cordate. Middle lobe is narrow toward its base. Lateral lobes are broad. Leaf margins are coarsely serrate. Leaf stalks are yellow with purple stains.
- Naturally small tree. Hardy. Ripens early.

Osborn's Prolific (Archipel, Neveralla)

- Medium to large fruit with dark, reddish-brown skin and amber flesh, often tinged pink. Best fresh. Light breba crop. Main crop on long (1"), slender stalk. Productive. Does well in most climates. Can split in high humidity.
- Leaves 3 to 5 lobed, the basal lobe sometimes auricled. Upper sinuses are medium depth and width, lower sinuses are shallow, and basal sinuses sometimes narrow and almost closed, but generally open, forming a cordate base. Leaf margins coarsely crenate.
- Productive tree, upright and naturally dwarf. Early ripening. Good for short-season, cool-summer regions.

Verte (Green Ischia)

- Small, grass-green fruit has dark, strawberry pulp. Fairly well-closed eye. Shrivels when ripe. Good breba crop.
- Leaves are medium size, glossy above, non-lobed to 3 lobed with shallow upper sinuses. Leaf base is broadly subcordate to truncate. Margins are coarsely crenate.
- Small tree. Fairly hardy. Matures late so not recommended for short-summer climates.

Verte

6

MATCHING METHODS AND VARIETIES TO KINDS OF COLD CLIMATES

FIG REGION 1 Frigid winters, hot summers		
Method #1	√	• Breba crop possible if you can maneuver a plant with long stems of previous year's growth into and out of winter quarters. • Good with dwarf varieties.
Method #2	√	• Same as for Method #1
Method #3	X	
Method #4	√	• Success if buried deep enough
Method #5	√	• Greenhouse: Varieties with closed eyes, such as Alma, Excel, Celeste, LSU Purple, and Verte, will be more resistant to spoilage organisms in the high humidity of a greenhouse.
	√	• Hoop house: Depending on hoop house size and depth of winter cold, additional heat or additional layer of winter protection, such as a blanket, over plants may be needed. • Varieties with closed eyes, such as Alma, Excel, Celeste, LSU Purple, and Verte, will be more resistant to spoilage organisms in the high humidity of a hoop house.

FIG REGION 2		
Frigid winters, cool summers		
Method #1	√	• Breba crop possible if you can maneuver a plant with some long stems of previous year's growth into and out of winter quarters. Depending on variety and length and temperature of growing season, it may only be possible to ripen a breba crop, in which case choose from varieties such as Black Mission, Desert King, Lattarula, and Verte, which bear good breba crops. • Good with dwarf varieties, possibly short season main varieties. • Pinching tips may help for main crop. • In summer, move to location with warmest and sunniest microclimate.
Method #2	√	• Same as for Method #1
Method #3	X	
Method #4	√	• Success if buried deep enough but probably have to choose variety for breba crop only, varieties such as Black Mission, Desert King, Lattarula, and Verte. • Pinching tips may help for main crop. • Plant where summer microclimate gathers extra warmth such as south-facing slopes and near walls or paving.
Method #5	√	• Greenhouse: Varieties with closed eyes, such as Alma, Excel, Celeste, LSU Purple, and Verte, will be more resistant to spoilage organisms in the high humidity of a greenhouse.
	√	• Hoop house: Depending on hoop house size and depth of winter cold, may need some additional heat or additional layer of winter protection over plants. • Varieties with closed eyes, such as Alma, Excel, Celeste, LSU Purple, and Verte, will be more resistant to spoilage organisms in the high humidity of a greenhouse.

FIG REGION 3 Coldish winters, cool summer		
Method #1	X	• Could be used but not necessary to grow in pot because plants are more or less cold-hardy in these regions.
Method #2	X	• Not needed
Method #3	X	• Not needed
Method #4	√	• Wrap plant using material and amount of wrapping according to expected degree of cold. • Train plant to 2 or 3 trunks to provide insurance in case atypical cold temperatures cause die back but spare 1 or 2 of them. Pinching tips may help advance ripening for long-season main crop varieties.
Method #5	√	• Not necessary unless an extra early harvest is wanted, to ripen a very late season main crop variety, or to ripen in warmth a variety that needs warmth for best quality fruit flavor.

7

PESTS

$\mathcal{F}$IGS ARE RELATIVELY PEST-FREE PLANTS, especially in cold winter climates. Still, as on most plants, pests do occasionally rear their ugly heads.

The main threats to outdoor plants are other animals who also enjoy the fruits, most notably birds, squirrels, bees, and wasps. The threats from birds and squirrels depends, to some extent, on the proximity of the plants to your terrace or wherever else you frequent, and what other creatures roam your estate. Here on my farmden, two dogs keep squirrels at a distance (usually), and birds don't seem to be a problem.

Depending on the variety of fig, very humid and rainy weather could cause ripe fruits to rot. Varieties with tougher skins and closed eyes are more rot resistant. "Tougher skins" might not sound appetizing for a fig, but one of my favorite varieties, Kadota, has a very appealing, chewy skin.

In a greenhouse, figs are similarly pest-free—usually. A few years ago, I began to notice white, cottony tufts on the fruits, leaves, and stems of my greenhouse figs. Mealybugs. The problem became bad enough to ruin the crop.

Mealybug on fig leaf

Repeated sprays of dormant oil or neem oil would be effective at keeping mealybugs at bay. This was not a viable solution in my greenhouse because growing beneath the fig trees in winter and early spring are beds of lettuce, mâche, celery, arugula, and other winter salad greens. Some research led me to two predators of these pests, *Chrysoperla rufilabris* ("green lacewing") and *Cryptolaemus montrouzieri* (with the good common name of "mealybug destroyer"), both of which I ordered online and released into the greenhouse. They were expensive, bringing the cost of my fresh figs to about one dollar each. Still worth it, though. I screened the greenhouse in an effort to perennialize these predators there.

Success: Mealybugs did not reappear.

Then scale insects, closely related to mealybugs, showed up, with the same effect. Scale insects look like $\frac{1}{16}$ inch (1.6 mm) diameter bumps on stems, leaves, or fruits. The "bumps" can be flicked off with your fingernail, which is satisfying *mano a mano* control unless you have oodles of them, which I soon did.

Scale insects are among those insects—aphids are another—that are "farmed" by ants. In return, ants get to dine on the sweet honeydew the insects excrete. My tack this time was, first, to rid the fig plants of as many scale insects as possible. This was when I started training my plants as espaliers, as described previously. As an espalier, each plant would have only one connection—its trunk—with the ground. I put a roadblock on the ant highway up from the ground by wrapping each plant's trunk with a band of masking tape coated with Tanglefoot®, a material that remains sticky for months on end.

With nothing more than a trunk and one or two permanent horizontal arms, a dormant espalier is relatively easy to scrub with an old toothbrush, repeatedly dipped in alcohol. Or, spray alcohol on portions of a plant at a time, then scrub them with a vegetable brush. The alcohol scrubs would kill a lot of scale insects; just in case any escaped the treatment, I

Scale insects on fig stem

Repelling ants with cinnamon on the ground and sticky band on the trunk

sometimes resort to sprays of dormant or neem oil, covering the salad greens each time to keep the spray off them. Anyway, the winter greens in the greenhouse start to give way to outdoor greens once spring moves along.

Currently, scrubbing pruned stems early in the season and, later in the season releasing predators, has kept mealybugs and scale insects sufficiently at bay—but controlling them is a work in progress.

In recent years, a new pest has reared its ugly head: spotted wing drosophila, know unaffectionately as SWD. Remembering back to high school biology, you might recognize "drosophila" as a fruit fly. Fruit flies are small flies who like to feast on ripe and overripe fruits. SWD is worse than the run-of-the-mill fruit fly; it feeds on fruits even before they are ripe.

Although I know of other greenhouse fig growers who have been plagued by SWD, this pest has not been a problem for my figs (yet?). The screening I put up in my greenhouse to keep my beneficial mealybug predators from escaping may be keeping SWD at bay, although my outdoor, potted figs (Method #1) also seem unaffected. Perhaps unscreened greenhouses provide overwintering sites for SWD or an unsuitable environment for some natural predator.

Cryptolaemus montrouzieri,
"mealybug destroyer"

Various organic sprays, such as Entrust, summer oil, and oxidate, can be effective against SWD, although spraying does take some of the fun out of growing and eating figs. And there are other approaches. For instance, eggs and larvae within harvested fruit can be killed by 3 days of refrigeration.

SWD attacks a number of fruits, especially berries, including my outdoor highbush blueberries. So far, my preferred and successful method of SWD control on outdoor berries is trapping. A number of bait and kill traps have been developed. The ones I have used are under development by Peter Jentsch, at Cornell University, and consist of a red gel infused with raspberry essence, which is attractive to SWD, and boric acid, which is toxic to them. Hanging one trap per blueberry plant provides control as long as the bait attractant is refreshed with a spray bottle of the raspberry-boric acid mix once or twice a week. I expect the treatment would be equally successful with figs, should SWD become a problem.

Nematodes are another possibility for controlling SWD. These microscopic, wormlike creatures are found throughout the world. Many are plant pests; many are beneficial. Nematodes sold for pest control usually need to be re-applied annually, but researchers at Cornell University (Dr. Elson Shields' laboratory) have isolated and propagated a few kinds of beneficial, perennialized nematodes that attack a variety of plant pests in the soil-inhabiting phase of their life cycle. I am trying them out for outdoor crops, such as root vegetables and fruit crops. I plan to introduce them into the greenhouse as a prophylactic measure.

Another potential, but usually not serious, pest of figs is the disease fig rust. The name tells the description: rusty areas on the leaves. This disease, like many fungal diseases, needs moisture, in this case a leaf surface that stays wet for 14 hours. So rust is not a problem in a greenhouse or hoop house but could be one on an outdoor fig. The weather can't be changed but the microclimate within a tree can be, by pruning so that all branches are bathed in light and air, which is good for quicker drying of leaves.

Keeping weed growth under control near the base of a plant also reduces humidity to help control rust, as does cleaning up diseased leaves that have fallen or, if heavily infected, are on the plant. But to reiterate, fig rust is usually not serious, and often can be ignored.

One more potential pest: Fig mosaic virus, the symptoms of which are yellowed or pale green areas on leaves whose edges blend in with healthy-looking, green areas, rather than being sharply differentiated from them. The discoloration could be as random mottling or as a pattern. Fruits on infected trees may be smaller, misshapen, and less abundant.

No cure exists for fig mosaic virus but there are ways to limit its arrival and spread. Get rid of any plants showing symptoms of the disease. The variety Black Mission is particularly susceptible; Alma, and other varieties that are hybrids involving *F. palmata*, are particularly resistant. Don't propagate new plants from infected plants, either by grafting or cuttings; those stems will carry the disease. The virus is not transmitted via seeds.

Fig mosaic virus

Some fig plants can coexist with the virus, bearing and growing well in spite of the infection.

The virus is also moved from plant to plant with the eriophyid mite *Aceria fici*. Oil or sulfur sprays can control mites but fig mosaic virus could be transmitted by even a single mite feeding. Plus, spraying is no fun, especially for a plant that otherwise is mostly pest-free. I suggest sacrificing any debilitated, infected plant, getting a new plant, and keeping on the lookout for any symptoms of the disease.

San Piero fig, main crop

8

HARVEST & PRESERVATION

𝒶 FULLY RIPE FIG IS A FRAGILE, perishable delicacy. And fully ripe is when it must be harvested for very best flavor; no further ripening will occur once a fruit has been separated from a branch. Fruits ready for harvest will droop, soften, and sometimes have a "tear" in their eye.

We cold-climate fig growers get very excited about seeing little figlets developing in the axils of the plants' leaves. But we must be patient because after their initial swelling, those small figs seem to just sit there forever. The fruits growth could be characterized by a sigmoidal growth curve, with a sharp initial increase (the hopeful phase) followed by a flattening (where impatience sets in) and then another rapid increase in size and weight, as well as sugars, coupled with softening and a change in color (the reward phase). Breba crops ripen pretty much all at once, and go through all three stages relatively fast. Main crop figs, as mentioned previously, ripen beginning with the oldest fruits at the proximal ends of stems and progressing sequentially towards the distal ends of the stems.

Depending on the length of your growing season and the variety of fig, some number of the youngest fruit will not ripen. If

A tear in its eye shows this fig is ready for eating

Fig latex

Fig stems, leaves, and unripe fruits, when cut, exude a white latex. One component of this latex is ficin, which is a proteolytic enzyme that can cause dermatitis. Avoid letting the white fluid drip on your skin when pruning, and don't eat unripe figs. It may be wise to wear gloves when harvesting lots of figs.

On the positive side, this fig latex was used as a color fixative for paint by Leonardo da Vinci.

This white, irritating latex exudes from cuts on fig stems, leaves, or unripe fruits

you fear figs not ripening, or not enough ripening, you can do something about it.

Ripening of nearly ripe figs can be hastened by "oiling the eye," which is just what it sounds like. Put a drop of olive oil on the eye (the opening opposite the stem end of the fruit). I tried this once as the fig season was drawing to a close. The fruit did ripen but flavor seemed to suffer some. Then again, the fig season was drawing to a close; cooler temperatures and less sunlight also could have accounted for less flavorful figs.

From midsummer on, warm, sunny weather obviates any need to hasten fruit ripening. That time of year does necessitate daily harvest—not an unpleasant demand.

Make the most of your FIGurative efforts (sorry 'bout that, I couldn't resist) by dealing with your harvest in the best possible way. The fresh fruit travels very well arm's length, that is, from plant right to mouth. At any rate, eat it soon. Fully ripe figs are not only very delicious but also very perishable.

Only when I have more figs than I could possibly eat do I conjure up other ways to use them. I've dried some by halving them and placing them in a dehydrator. They dried and then stored well... but, I must admit, did not taste that good. Other varieties than the (unnamed) one I used might do better. Most commercial, dried figs, which I do enjoy (except during fresh fig season here), are of the variety Calimyrna (Lob Injir), a Smyrna type fig that requires pollination and is suitable only for Mediterranean-type climates.

I mostly grow fruits to eat fresh. My most complicated fig recipe is to eat the fruit with some super-dark chocolate. Mmmmm. Perhaps with a touch of some liqueur.

I'll close this chapter with a quote from a poem, entitled "Figs," by D. H. Lawrence, "The proper way to eat a fig, in society / Is to split it in four, holding it by the stump / And open it, so that it is a glittering, rosy, moist, honied, heavy-petalled four-petalled flower."

Tsk. Tsk. Those Brits. Very poetic, but I don't eat my figs this way.

A drop of oil in fig's "eye"
speeds ripening

9

FUTURE DIRECTIONS

WHEN I LEFT WISCONSIN, with my potted fig tree and many other fruit trees in tow, I moved to southern Delaware, a much warmer climate. Perfect for planting a fig tree out in open ground, right? No, not in those days.

In the decades since that move, winter and summer temperatures have inched upwards. Back when I lived in Delaware, winters were cold enough that planting a fig in the ground even that far south was unheard of, so unheard of that Professor Ira Condit, one of the foremost researchers and writers on figs from the University of California in the first half of the 20th century, deemed it worthy to visit "a small commercial planting [of figs] ... on the place of Stoughton Sterling, Crisfield, Maryland." Fifty miles to my south and proximity to water made it possible—but just barely so—for Stoughton to grow figs commercially outdoors. I did find the Sterling Farm about 30 years after Dr. Condit's visit. The site, overgrown and with decrepit trees, was reminiscent of a Mississippi bayou. Ms. Sterling, Stoughton's wife, did recall the visit from "some professor from California."

Trees in my collection soon expanded to over two dozen varieties, in pots in Delaware and, a few years later when I moved to

Maryland, in open ground. To carry the plants through winters in Maryland, it was necessary to bend stems to the ground and then cover them with insulation.

Not so these days. Trees now thrive planted outdoors not only in Maryland and southern Delaware but also as far north as New Jersey and warmer parts of New York, such as Brooklyn and Long Island. As our planet warms further, I may one day be planting my fig trees in open ground here on my farmden in New York's Hudson Valley!

Until that day arrives, I'll continue to use various techniques to be able to enjoy fresh, homegrown figs. And I'll continue to think about better ways to grow them.

For instance, the espalier method of pruning that I now use for my greenhouse figs, described in Method #5, has potential to be adapted to further expand the fig-growing repertoire.

The downside to the system, as I described it, is that the pruning, while quick and straightforward, pretty much eliminates the breba crop. And two of the varieties that I prune this way do, in fact, bear very good breba crops when allowed. I'm experimenting with getting that crop as well, by pruning at the end of the season so as to leave every other shoot at a length of about a foot. That leaves some one-year-old wood for the earlier crop. The following year I plan to leave foot-long shoots wherever shoots were totally cut back the previous year. The year after that year I'll alternate them the way they were the first year, and so on, year after year.

So far, the technique has yielded only limited success. Some years, some brebas have developed, but not that many. Sometimes none. Pruning off any main crop figs just as they start to develop near the base of a new shoot might instead induce buds there to develop into brebas the following spring.

Brebas do sometimes develop near or at the far end of one-year-old stems. Perhaps this is variety dependent. To allow those brebas to develop would require leaving the full length of stem.

Espalier fig with breba ripening on old wood as new crop forms on new shoots

I could leave every other stem, or perhaps every third stem, at its full length and then, right after the breba figs are harvested, cut those stems down to their origin, or to some vigorous side-shoot growing off lower along the stem. Those vigorous stems could go on to bear a main crop, which might be possible in the long growing season within the greenhouse.

And perhaps I'll be harvesting ripe figs from in-the-ground plants outdoors sooner than expected. To that end, I'm trying variations on my greenhouse espalier technique outdoors. My farmden's climate of frigid winters and hot summers would call for a main crop variety, preferably one not ripening too late in the season.

Training and growing is the same as previously described for my espaliered greenhouse figs except that the horizontal branches—the cordons—are trained near, at, or even below below ground level.

Espalier fig outdoors, trained low

For a plant trained right at ground level, I cut the whole plant back to near ground level its first winter. Of the many shoots that arise the following spring, one (or two, going in opposite directions; or four, radiating out in an X pattern, depending on ground space available) is selected growing out near ground level and its base of each stem or stems is pinned down to keep it low. These will be permanent cordons. Remove any others.

Leave the far portion of any stem free; it will naturally curl upwards, which keeps it growing vigorously. (Vertical stems, whether oriented that way naturally or through training, are inherently more vigorous than horizontal stems.) But pin down the more proximal portion of any cordon-to-be as it grows.

Each fall, whether cordons are slightly above ground, at ground level, or below ground level, cut all those vertical stems back to the cordon, and once a cordon itself has grown as long as desired, shorten it back to where it began growing that season.

Training fig along the ground for winter cold protection

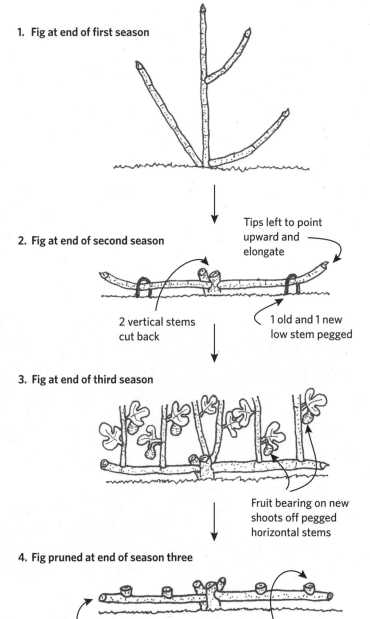

1. **Fig at end of first season**

2. **Fig at end of second season**

Tips left to point upward and elongate

2 vertical stems cut back

1 old and 1 new low stem pegged

3. **Fig at end of third season**

Fruit bearing on new shoots off pegged horizontal stems

4. **Fig pruned at end of season three**

Horizontals shortened because full length

All verticals cut close to horizontals

Come colder weather, with its vertical branches lopped back, it's easy to protect any low-trained fig plant against cold by heaping insulating material over it. Insulate the plant with a deep layer of wood chips, autumn leaves, sawdust, or any other fluffy mulch, and top the whole thing with a tarp to shed ,water. For the tree planted below ground level, rigid insulation or wood (old doors?) could be laid over the trench upon which is heaped additional insulating material.

As with the previously described Method #4 for overwintering a fig, protection is needed from rodents: wait until consistent below freezing temperatures before covering; paint or spray trunks with repellent; trap; enlist the services of one or more cats.

Cordons trained slightly above ground level could also be protected by the system of wire hoops and clear plastic that I use for

Low espalier fig outdoors, insulated and covered too keep out moisture

growing very early or very late crops of lettuce, arugula, and endive in my vegetable garden, topped with insulating mulch, if needed. In late winter or early spring, removing the insulation allows the sun to shine through the clear plastic to get the trees off to an earlier start, with some protection against cold. Remove any covering, unless it's clear plastic for an earlier start, before buds swell in spring. Remember, a thoroughly dormant fig plant is cold-hardy to about 20° F (-7° C), or lower, depending on the variety.

One way or another, now and into the future, I'll be harvesting fresh figs here in this cold climate. You can, too!

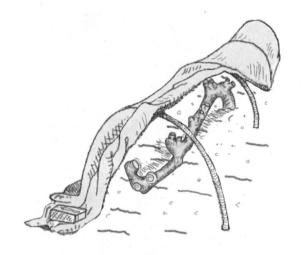

Outdoor fig espalier in low tunnel under clear plastic film

San Piero fig, main crop; delicious!

FURTHER INFORMATION

BOOKS

Benson, Martin. *Benson's Guide to Fig Culture in Open Ground in the North,* 1886.

Biggs, Steven. *Grow Figs Where You Think You Can't.* No Guff Press, 2012.

Chamberlain, John. "Figs in the North." *Garden Mag.* 29:238, 1919.

Condit, Ira. *The Fig,* 1947.

Condit, Ira. "Fig Varieties, A Monograph." *Hilgardia* 23(11):323-537, February 1955. https://ucanr.edu/datastoreFiles/391-296.pdf

Eisen, Gustave. *The Fig: Its History, Culture and Curing,* 1901.

Read, Stephen. *The Concise Book of Figs,* 2013. 40 pages.

Thompson, David. *A Guide to Growing Figs Under Glass,* 2011 (reprint of old booklet).

Worthington, James. *Manual of Fig Culture in the Northern and Middle States,* 1869.

Janick, Jules and James Moore (ed.) *Advances in Fruit Breeding.* Purdue University Press, 1975.

WEBSITES & SOURCES FOR PLANTS

arboreumco.com

crfg.org

figs4fun.com

mountainfigs.net

ourfigs.com

onegreenworld.com

planetfig.com

raintreenursery.com

theitaliangardenproject.com

treesofjoy.com

FIG FACEBOOK GROUPS

European Figs

Fig Addiction

Fig Collectors

Fig Culture

Fig Hunters and Figger Friends

Figs and Gigs Inc. Fig Tree Group

Figs Figs Figs

Figs Gardening 101

Figworld

Northeast Fig Growers

Northern Fig Growers

Rafeds Fig Group

The Original Fig Variety Database

Upstate New York Fig Growers

Vinny figs

INDEX

ABOUT THE AUTHOR

*L*EE REICH, PHD, dove into gardening decades ago, initially with one foot in academia as an agricultural scientist with the USDA and then Cornell University, and one foot in the field, the organic field. He eventually expanded his field to a "farmden" (more than a garden, less than a farm) and left academia to lecture, consult, and write. He is author of many books, including *The Ever Curious Gardener, Weedless Gardening, The Pruning Book,* and *Landscaping with Fruit,* as well as a syndicated column for Associated Press. Lee has a PhD in Horticulture from the University of Maryland, and an MS in Soil Science and a BA in Chemistry from the University of Wisconsin. He blogs at leereich.com from his farmden in New Paltz, NY.

A NOTE ABOUT THE PUBLISHER

New Society Publishers is an activist, solutions-oriented publisher focused on publishing books to build a more just and sustainable future. Our books offer tips, tools, and insights from leading experts in a wide range of areas.

We're proud to hold to the highest environmental and social standards of any publisher in North America. When you buy New Society books, you are part of the solution!

At New Society Publishers, we care deeply about *what* we publish—but also about *how* we do business.

- All our books are printed on 100% post-consumer recycled paper, processed chlorine-free, with low-VOC vegetable-based inks (since 2002). We print all our books in North America (never overseas)
- Our corporate structure is an innovative employee shareholder agreement, so we're one-third employee-owned (since 2015)
- We've created a Statement of Ethics (2021). The intent of this Statement is to act as a framework to guide our actions and facilitate feedback for continuous improvement of our work
- We're carbon-neutral (since 2006)
- We're certified as a B Corporation (since 2016)
- We're Signatories to the UN's Sustainable Development Goals (SDG) Publishers Compact (2020–2030, the Decade of Action)

To download our full catalog, sign up for our quarterly newsletter, and to learn more about New Society Publishers, please visit newsociety.com

ENVIRONMENTAL BENEFITS STATEMENT

New Society Publishers saved the following resources by printing the pages of this book on chlorine free paper made with 100% post-consumer waste.

TREES	WATER	ENERGY	SOLID WASTE	GREENHOUSE GASES
26	2,100	11	90	11,310
FULLY GROWN	GALLONS	MILLION BTUs	POUNDS	POUNDS

Environmental impact estimates were made using the Environmental Paper Network Paper Calculator 4.0. For more information visit www.papercalculator.org

Certified B Corporation

new society PUBLISHERS
www.newsociety.com

FSC
www.fsc.org
MIX
Paper from responsible sources
FSC® C016245

SDG PUBLISHERS COMPACT